The Economic Basis
of Politics

Charles A. Beard.

The Economic Basis
of Politics

by
Charles A. Beard

New York
Alfred · A · Knopf
1923

Set up, electrotyped, and printed by the Vail-Ballou Co., Binghamton, N. Y.
Paper furnished by W. F. Etherington & Co., New York.
Bound by the H. Wolff Estate, New York.

MANUFACTURED IN THE UNITED STATES OF AMERICA

112941

Prefatory Note

This little volume is composed of four lectures which I gave at Amherst College in 1916 on the Clark Foundation. They are reproduced as delivered except for minor changes and for a revision of the fourth lecture in the light of recent political experience. The reasons for occasional repetitions are therefore apparent.

CHARLES A. BEARD.

New Milford, Conn.,
October 5, 1921.

Contents

I

The Doctrines of the Philosophers

T HE founders of this lectureship desire to help carry forward the eternal quest of mankind for ways and means with which to control its social destiny for noble ends. Some of the most splendid traditions of the race are associated with this search. The mystic Plato, the sagacious Aristotle, the gentle Sir Thomas More, and the courageous Condorcet, to mention none nearer our time, sought far and wide for the key to the great mystery. The fruits of their labors are a priceless heritage.

The imperious Burke likewise thought the theme worthy of his talents, but he soon gave it up, confessing defeat. "I doubt," he says, "whether the history of mankind is yet complete enough, if it ever can be so, to furnish ground for a sure theory on the internal causes which necessarily affect the fortune of a state. I am far from denying the operation of such causes: but they are infinitely uncertain, and much more obscure and much more difficult to trace than

the foreign causes that tend to raise, to de-
press, and sometimes to overwhelm a community. It is often impossible, in these political
inquiries, to find any proportion between the
apparent force of any moral causes we may
assign and their known operation. We are
therefore obliged to deliver up that operation to mere chance, or, more piously (perhaps, more rationally), to the occasional inter-
position and irresistible hand of the Great
Disposer." In short, confronted by the complex and bewildering facts of social life, Burke
cries aloud, with the mediaeval priest overwhelmed by the horror of the Black Death,
"Deus vult."

In the field of natural science, such a confes-
sion is a plea of intellectual bankruptcy. In
that sphere persistent and penetrating research,
relentless and unafraid, brings about the pro-
gressive conquest and subjugation of the material world. Indeed the very research in mechanics and chemistry that produced the machine age has torn asunder the foundations of
the old social order, released new and terrify-
ing forces, and now threatens the dissolution
of society itself. The present plight of the
world seems to show that mankind is in the
grip of inexorable forces which may destroy

Doctrines of the Philosophers

civilization if not subdued to humane purposes.
It may be that in the end we must, with Burke,
confess the futility of our quest. Even then
we shall say with Heine:

> Also fragen wir beständig
> Bis man uns mit einer Handvoll
> Erde endlich stopft die Mäuler,
> Aber ist das eine Antwort?

So the eternal search goes on. At the very
outset the seekers are confronted by two conflicting theories concerning the problem itself.
These are summed up by John Stuart Mill at
the opening of his famous work on representative government. According to one of them,
government, namely, human control, is merely
a problem in invention, of determining what is
best and adapting our means to the desired
end. According to the other theory, government is not a matter of human choice at all
but an inevitable, natural growth in which the
purposes of man have no part.

Each of these doctrines, we must admit with
Mill, is untenable if pushed to an exclusive and
logical conclusion; yet somewhere in between
them lies important truth. Long the victim
of material forces, man has, by taking thought,
made himself master of wind and wave and

storm. May he not, by taking thought, lift himself above the social conflicts that destroy civilizations and make himself master of his social destiny? Perhaps not; but as the human mind is greater than the waterfall which it compels or the lightning's flash which it confines, so the control of human destiny is a nobler object of inquiry than the search for material power. Even though every door be slammed in our faces, still must we knock.

As the theme is old, we, as humble students, must, of necessity, first survey the conclusions of the great masters who have gone on before. We must first find out what they thought about the nature of the forces which are responsible for the origins, forms, and changes of political institutions.

At the beginning of such an inquiry we face, of course, the mighty Aristotle, "the master of all them that know." He rightly deserves to be called "the father of political science" because he took it out of the sphere of utopian idealism where Plato left it and placed it on the strong foundation of natural history. As Oncken rightly says, it was the use of the methods of natural science in his inductive studies that enabled Aristotle to make his great contribution to Greek thought. He was the son

Doctrines of the Philosophers

of a doctor who had written many books on medicine and physiology and he was himself no mean student of morphology and anatomy. Moreover he combined practical experience in politics with long and wide-reaching researches in the history of human institutions. It is for these reasons, perhaps, that Aristotle stood midway between those who thought that human society was a mechanism to be refashioned at will and those who accepted good and ill as fatalities of the gods. At all events we know that he sought to combine the idealism of ethics with the realism of historical research.

The most striking thing about Aristotle's *Politics* is the sharp contrast which it presents to most modern books on the same subject. The latter deal mainly with the structure and forms of government, the machinery and methods of elections, the powers and duties of public officers. The texture of society itself is left to the sociologist. The production and distribution of wealth, the foundations of human life, are assigned to the economist.

The reasons for this somewhat arbitrary carving up of the social organism for the purposes of study are not difficult to discover.

The Economic Basis of Politics

Adam Smith and the older writers spoke of "Political Economy." About the middle of the nineteenth century, thinkers in that field were mainly concerned with formulating a mill owner's philosophy of society; and mill owners resented every form of state interference with their "natural rights." So "political economy" became "economics." The state was regarded as a badge of original sin, not to be mentioned in economic circles. Of course, it was absurd for men to write of the production and distribution of wealth apart from the state which defines, upholds, taxes, and regulates property, the very basis of economic operations; but absurdity does not restrain the hand of the apologist.

To this simple historical explanation must be added another. This is an age of intense specialization. Every field of human knowledge is so vast that the workers therein are driven, in their endeavour to see things as they really are, further and further into the details of their subject. They then easily forget the profound truth enunciated by Buckle that the science of any subject is not at its centre but at its periphery where it impinges upon all other sciences. So the living organism of human society as a subject of inquiry has

Doctrines of the Philosophers

been torn apart and parcelled out among specialists.

Aristotle, by contrast, combines economics, politics and ethics. He considers the nature and function of the family before he takes up the forms of state. He then moves to the subject of property in its human relationships and considers the limits of communism and individualism. He rejects the former as impossible but he tells us that "poverty is the parent of revolution and crime." At no time does he lose sight of ethics. The aim of the family and of property, as of the state, is the best life. Property as a means of getting more property or as an end in itself is inconceivable to him as a philosopher. Its aim is to enable man to live temperately and well, and this aim should determine the amount which each citizen ought to hold.

Having surveyed the family and property and the production and distribution of wealth, —the texture of society—Aristotle proceeds to the consideration of the forms and nature of government, the causes of revolutions, and the conditions which favour the best society of which human nature is capable. How sound is this, how wise, how much more scientific than our modern practice of dissection and

[15]

The Economic Basis of Politics

distribution among specialists! So the first conclusion to be drawn from Aristotle is that he never for an instant dreamed that ethics, politics, and economics could be torn apart and treated as separate subjects. He would have said of such pseudo-sciences with Ruskin: "I simply am uninterested in them as I should be in a science of gymnastics which assumed that men had no skeletons. It might be shown on that supposition that it would be advantageous to roll students up into pellets, flatten them into cakes, or stretch them into cables; and that when these results were effected the re-insertion of the skeleton would be attended with various inconveniences to their constitutions." Aristotle simply could not imagine a treatise on the state that did not consider the whole man rather than a highly hypothetical man—man as a mere political animal. This is apparent in his treatment of every phase of his subject.

When he approaches the heart of the matter, namely, the causes of variations in the forms of the state, he immediately relates economics and politics. He declares that there must "necessarily be as many different forms of government as there are ranks in the society, arising from the superiority of some over others and their different situations. And

Doctrines of the Philosophers

these seem to be two, as they say of the winds: namely, the north and the south; and all the others are declinations from these. And thus in politics, there is the government of the many and the government of the few; or a democracy and an oligarchy. . . . A democracy is a state where the freemen and the poor, being the majority, are invested with the power of the state. An oligarchy is a state where the rich and those of noble families, being few, possess it." In commenting on this laconic explanation of the differences in the form of the state by reference to differences in wealth, Aristotle's distinguished editor, Jowett, remarks in an equally laconic fashion: "As the poor or the middle class, or the notables predominate, they divide the government among themselves."

As economic classes depend upon the character and distribution of property, and as the forms of state turn upon the predominance of classes, it would follow logically that alterations in the form of state must have some connection with the changing fortunes of classes. This is exactly the conclusion Aristotle reached after he had considered the forces and conditions which produce revolutions in the affairs of nations. "Political revolutions," he says,

The Economic Basis of Politics

"spring from a disproportionate increase in any part of the state. . . . When the rich grow numerous or properties increase, the form of government changes into an oligarchy or a government of families. . . . Revolutions break out when opposite parties, e. g. the rich and poor, are equally balanced and there is little or nothing between them. . . . Revolutions in democracies are generally caused by the intemperance of demagogues who either in their private capacity lay information against rich men until they compel them to combine (for a common danger unites even the bitterest enemies) or, coming forward in public, stir up the people against them. The truth of this remark is proved by a variety of examples. At Cos the democracy was overthrown because wicked demagogues arose and the notables combined. . . . The democracy at Heraclea was overthrown shortly after the foundation of the colony by the injustice of the demagogues which drove out the notables, who came back in a body and put an end to the democracy." There are collateral and incidental causes of revolutions, but "the universal and chief cause" of revolutionary feeling is "the desire of equality, when men think they are equal to others who have more than themselves; or again, the

Doctrines of the Philosophers

desire of inequality and superiority when, conceiving themselves to be superior, they think they have not more but the same or less than their inferiors; pretensions which may or may not be just."

It can hardly be doubted that Aristotle, in spite of some confusion of thought, looks upon the character and distribution of wealth in society as the chief determining factors in fixing the form of state. It is equally clear that he finds the causes of revolutions in states in contests among those who have much, those who have little, and those who have no, property. This disparity in fortune is the fundamental condition of which the demagogue avails himself in order to stir up strife and overturn established orders. Another commentator, Mr. A. D. Lindsay, observes: "When we come to Aristotle's analysis of existing constitutions we find that while he regards them as imperfect approximations to the ideal, he also thinks of them as the result of struggles between classes. . . . And each class is thought of, not as trying to express an ideal, but as struggling to acquire power to maintain its position. . . . His analysis of the facts forces him to look upon them [the Greek states] as the scene of struggling factions. The causes of revolutions are not described as primarily changes in the conception of the common good, but changes in the military or economic power of the several classes in the state."

Having come, by an inductive study, to the conclusion that there is a fundamental relation between the form and fortunes of the state and the character and distribution of property among the population, Aristotle applies the doctrine in his inquiry into "what is the best constitution for most states and the best life for most men, neither assuming a standard of virtue which is above ordinary persons, nor an education which is exceptionally favoured by nature and circumstances, nor yet an ideal state which is an aspiration only."

His opinion touching this point is clear and simple: "Now in all states there are three elements; one class is very rich, another very poor, and a third is a mean. It is admitted that moderation and the mean are best, and therefore it will clearly be best to possess the gifts of fortune in moderation; for in that condition of life men are most ready to listen to reason. . . . Those who have too much of the goods of fortune, strength, wealth, friends, and the like are neither willing nor able to submit to authority. . . . On the other hand, the very poor, who are in the opposite extreme, are too degraded. So that the one class cannot obey and can only rule despotically; the other knows not how to command and must be ruled like slaves. Thus arises a city not of freemen but of masters and slaves, the one despising, the other envying. . . . A city ought to be composed, as far as possible, of equals and similars; and these are generally the middle classes. Wherefore a city which is composed of middle class citizens is necessarily best governed; they are, as we say, the natural elements of a state. And this is the class of citizens which is most secure in a state, for they do not, like the poor, covet their neighbour's goods; nor do others covet theirs, as the poor covet the goods of the rich; and as they neither plot against others, nor are themselves plotted against, they pass through life safely."

When Aristotle takes up the problem of finding the best material for a democracy he is no less insistent upon the economic element as the fundamental factor. The safest and most enduring form of democracy is, in his opinion, that based upon agriculture. In such a state the people are compelled to work hard for a livelihood, they have little time for political intrigue and combinations, they do not covet

The Economic Basis of Politics

the property of others, and they will endure in
patience oligarchies or tyrannies if they are allowed to work and are not deprived of their
lands or cattle. Next to an agricultural democracy, that of a pastoral people is best, for
those who live by their flocks are in many ways
similar to husbandmen and they are well fitted
for war. The worst and most dangerous democracy of all is that founded on commerce,
for there is no moral excellence in the employments of traders, mechanics and labourers.
By virtue of their economic occupations, they
are turbulent, instable, and easily the prey of
demagogues. [1]

[1] "The best material of democracy is an agricultural population; there is no difficulty in forming a democracy where the
mass of the people live by agriculture or tending of cattle.
Being poor, they have no leisure and therefore do not often
attend the assembly, and not having the necessaries of
life they are always at work, and do not covet the property
of others. . . . Next best to an agricultural and in many
respects similar are a pastoral people, who live by their
flocks; they are the best trained of any for war, robust
in body, and able to camp out. The people of whom other
democracies consist are far inferior to them, for their life
is inferior; there is no room for moral excellence in any
of their employments, whether they be mechanics, traders,
or labourers. . . . The last form of democracy, that in which
all share alike, is one which cannot be born by all states, and
will not last long unless well regulated by laws and customs.
The most general causes which tend to destroy this or
other kinds of government have now been pretty fully considered." Here Aristotle evidently refers to Bk. V. ch. 5
where he ascribes revolutions in democracies to hatred
stirred by demagogues against the rich.

Doctrines of the Philosophers

As Aristotle, first among the ancients, commands the attention of every student of politics, so Machiavelli, first among the moderns, arrests our interest. Like his Greek predecessor, he was a man of affairs and a painstaking searcher into the history of political institutions. During most of his active life he was in the public service of Florence. He was familiar with the inner politics of the turbulent Italian states. To experience in domestic politics he added a knowledge of foreign affairs gathered from many difficult diplomatic negotiations and missions. As his voluminous writings attest, he was a profound student of history, politics, and diplomacy.

When he writes of states founded upon the sword, his task is simple. He has merely to reckon with military forces and devices. When he deals with the origins of civil principalities he follows in the path cut by Aristotle. "A principality," he says, "results either from the will of the people or that of the nobles according as one or the other prevails. For the nobles, seeing that they cannot resist the people, begin to have recourse to the influence and reputation of one of their own class, and make him a prince, so that under the shadow of his power they may give free scope to their desires.

The Economic Basis of Politics

The people also seeing that they cannot resist the nobles, have recourse to the influence and reputation of one man and make him a prince so as to be protected by his authority."

In advising the prince, once established, how best to maintain his power, Machiavelli warns him to take account of the conflict of classes out of which political power springs and to balance one over against the other, leaning to the right or to the left as occasion demands. By this shifting of affections the prince can cause the passions and ambitions of each class to nullify those of the other and so keep himself secure in power. In times of peace even, the prince should give attention to the balance of classes. "As cities are generally divided into guilds and classes, he should keep account of these bodies and occasionally be present at their assemblies, and should set an example of his affability and magnificence; preserving however always the majesty of his dignity."

If time permitted it would be interesting to survey the political philosophies of Bacon, Raleigh, Harrington,[2] Montesquieu, Burke,

[2] More than a century after Machiavelli's death an English writer, James Harrington, in constructing his model commonwealth, *Oceana,* gave to idealists the same advice that Machiavelli gave to the prince, namely that they should take into account the fact that the forms and distribution

[24]

Doctrines of the Philosophers

and a score of other great men who have speculated upon the origin, nature, and fortunes of the state; but there is a limit to our enterprise. Students familiar with their writings know how deep is the impress of economics upon them.

Still there is one more philosopher of the Old World who cannot be neglected. As we have, of necessity, examined the opinions of Aristotle and Machiavelli, so must we, of equal necessity, look into the writings of John Locke. He was, in a serious way, the forerunner of the American and French revolutions as well as the supreme apologist for the English rev-

of property in society determine the nature of the state. "Dominion" he wrote, "is property, real or personal; that is to say, in lands, or in money and goods. Lands or the parts and parcels of a territory are held by the proprietor or proprietors, lord or lords of it, in some proportion; and such (except it be in a city that has little or no land and whose revenue is in trade) as is the proportion or balance or dominion or property in land, such is the nature of the empire. If one man be sole landlord or own three parts in four, the state is an absolute monarchy. If a few or a nobility with a clergy be the landlords and overbalance the people to a like proportion, the state is an oligarchy or a mixed monarchy. If the whole people be landlords or the lands are so divided among them that no man or aristocracy of men overbalance the many then the state is a commonwealth or anarchy." In short, political power follows property and it is the function of the statesman to see that property is not too narrowly concentrated, that a substantial landed class be maintained as the basis or stabilizer of the state.

[25]

The Economic Basis of Politics

olution of 1688. All the great French critics of the old régime from Voltaire to Condorcet were familiar with their Locke. His works were translated into French for the benefit of those not familiar with his native tongue. Everywhere in the English colonies in America, students of politics were also acquainted with the philosopher of the Glorious Revolution. From him Jefferson drew both inspiration and guidance. Parts of the Declaration of Independence are merely paraphrases of passages in Locke's *Two Treatises on Government.* Like Aristotle and Machiavelli, this English thinker combined literary pursuits with practical affairs, although it must be said that his first-hand experience with politics is not to be compared with that of the Italian or the Greek.

Both the origin and end of the state Locke finds in the roots of property. "To avoid these inconveniences which disorder men's property in the state of nature," he writes, "men unite into societies, that they may have the united strength of the whole society to secure and defend their properties and may have standing rules to bound it, by which every one may know what is his. . . . The reason why men enter into society is the preservation of their

Doctrines of the Philosophers

property, and the end why they choose and authorize a legislature is that there may be laws made and rules set as guards and fences to the properties of all the members of the society." As the origin of the state is to be found in the requirements of property owners, so is the end of the state to be sought in the same source. "The great and chief end, therefore, of men's uniting into commonwealths and putting themselves under government is the preservation of their property."

As the preservation of property is the origin and end of the state, so it gives the right of revolution against any government or authority that invades property. Such is the economic foundation of the ethics of revolt. "The supreme power cannot take from any man part of his property without his consent." If perchance this is done, the owners of property, the people, have the right to cast off the old form of government and to establish a new one that will observe the ends of civil society. This will not be undertaken, of course, for light and transient reasons, but when a long train of abuses menaces the privileges of property and person, the right of revolution may be exercised.

The Economic Basis of Politics

So far we have considered only Old World writers, and according to methods of thinking cherished in many quarters we might easily conclude that European philosophy has no application to us—a favoured people who live in a new dispensation of our own making. It cannot be denied that the social and economic conditions of Athens, feudal Europe, or the Stuart age were in many respects different from those prevailing in the United States. Still mankind here, as in the Old World, must struggle for existence and, allowing for the divergences in circumstances, we have no reason for assuming that the economic laws which governed in other times and other lands are without effect in this fortunate country. Certainly the founders of the American republic did not assume that in shaping our political institutions they could break with the experience and philosophy of the past. That will be discovered by any one who takes the trouble to read the records of the convention assembled at Philadelphia in 1787 to frame the Constitution of the United States.

Time does not permit even a casual survey of those voluminous documents. Nor is such a general inquiry necessary. By common con-

Doctrines of the Philosophers

sent it is recognized that James Madison was "the father of the Constitution." He was a profound student of history and government. He kept the most complete record of the debates in the federal convention that has come down to us. He spent his long life in public service and political activities. He was twice President of the American union, and was intimately acquainted with nearly all the great statesmen of his time. He was the adviser of Washington and the confidant of Jefferson. He knew at first hand the stuff of which governments are made. To a study such as we are now making his views are simply indispensable and he may speak for his contemporaries.

In a powerful essay written in defence of the Constitution of the United States—Number Ten of the Federalist,—Madison sums up his political science in such a clear and concise form that no one can mistake his meaning. The prime function of government, he says, is the protection of the different and unequal faculties of man for acquiring property. "From the protection of different and unequal faculties of acquiring property, the possession of different degrees and kinds of property im-

mediately results." This inexorable economic
fact is the basis of political fact. Madison
goes on: "From the influence of these [differ-
ent degrees and kinds of property] on the
sentiments and views of the respective proprietors ensues a division of society into
different interests and parties. The latent
causes of faction are thus sown in the nature
of man; and we see them everywhere brought
into different degrees of activity, according to
the different circumstances of civil society."
Thus, in the opinion of the Father of the
American Constitution, politics springs inevitably, relentlessly out of economics. The *sentiments* and *views* which arise from the possession of different degrees and kinds of property
form the stuff of so-called "political psychol-
ogy."

After this statement of controlling principle, Madison moves to his next fundamental
problem, namely, the effect of these differences
in economic condition and in political psychol-
ogy on the government and its operation.
Here too he has no doubts. He admits that
there are occasionally fanciful and frivolous
causes of internal disturbances but he is quick
to add that "the most common and durable

source of factions [3] has been the various and unequal distribution of property. Those who hold and those who are without property have ever formed distinct interests in society. Those who are creditors and those who are debtors fall under a like distinction. A landed interest, a manufacturing interest, a mercantile interest, with many lesser interests grow up of necessity in civilized nations and divide them into different classes actuated by different sentiments and views. The regulation of these various and interfering interests forms the principal task of modern legislation, and involves the spirit of party and faction in the necessary and ordinary operations of the government. . . . The causes of faction cannot be removed. . . . We well know that neither moral nor religious motives can be relied on as an adequate control."

Thus Madison holds that, owing to the nature of men, unequal distribution of property is unavoidable; that in every civilized society, there will be persons holding different kinds and amounts of property; that from their holdings will arise special sentiments and views;

[3] "Faction" was the common term in the eighteenth century for "political party."

that from these differing sentiments will arise
contending political parties; and that political
parties will seek to accumulate a majority and
control the state. This danger, majority rule,
Madison said in the constitutional convention,
was especially grave in view of the inevitable
rise of a landless proletariat—a vast class of
propertyless persons likely to be actuated by
the same sentiments and therefore certain to
assault the rights of the propertied classes.
To secure the public good and private rights
against the dangers of such a majority party
bent on attacking the property of the minority,
and at the same time preserve the spirit and
form of popular government, he concluded,
was the object toward which the framers of
the Constitution of the United States directed
their skill and their energies.

In short, the fundamental purposes and ideals
of a free government in the New World, by
the iron necessity of circumstances could not be
essentially different from those of the Old
World or the Ancient World. If government
here is different from government in other
times and places it is mainly because the forms
and distribution of property are different.

Doctrines of the Philosophers

But it may be said that Madison was from a slave state where political power did in fact result from the possession of land and slaves and that he was reading into universal politics the conclusions drawn from local accidents. Such a conclusion would of course be unjust to the great Virginian because all through his works there are the evidences of erudition which mark him out as one of the most learned men of his day. For a moment we may let the objection stand and inquire what were the views of some leading statesman and philosopher in the free North. Surely none will object if I choose a man who long and honorably represented the commonwealth of Massachustts in the Senate of the United States and who found imperishable fame in the annals of his country, Daniel Webster. In a speech of great cogency and learning, delivered in the constitutional convention of his state in 1820, he defended the distribution of representation in the Senate on the basis of property. The principle of representing property, he said, was well established by writers of the greatest authority. Then he went on to expound his views with a show of learning and philosophy not often displayed in the American constitutional discussions.

"Those who have treated of natural law have maintained," he said, "as a principle of that law, that, as far as the object of society is the protection of something in which the members possess unequal shares, it is just that the weight of each person in the common councils should bear a relation and proportion to his interest. Such is the sentiment of Grotius, and he refers, in support of it, to several institutions among the ancient states.

"Those authors who have written more particularly on the subject of political institutions have, many of them, maintained similar sentiments. Not, indeed, that every man's power should be in exact proportion to his property, but that, in a general sense, and in a general form, property, as such, should have its weight and influence in political arrangements. Montesquieu speaks with approbation of the early Roman regulation, made by Servius Tullius, by which the people were distributed into classes, according to their property, and the public burdens apportioned to each individual according to the degree of power which he possessed in the government. By this regu-

Doctrines of the Philosophers

lation, he observes, some bore with the greatness of their tax because of their proportionable participation in power and credit; others consoled themselves for the smallness of their power and credit by the smallness of their tax.

"One of the most ingenious of political writers is Mr. Harrington, an author not now read as much as he deserves. It is his leading object, in his *Oceana,* to prove, that power *naturally* and *necessarily* follows property. He maintains that a government founded on property is legitimately founded; and that a government founded on the disregard of property is founded in injustice, and can only be maintained by military force. 'If one man,' says he, 'be sole landlord, like the Grand Seignior, his empire is absolute. If a few possess the land, this makes the Gothic or feudal constitution. If the *whole people* be landlords, then it is a commonwealth.' 'It is strange,' says an ingenious person in the last century, 'that Harrington should be the first man to find out so evident and demonstrable a truth as that of property being the true basis and *measure* of power.' In truth, he was not the first. The idea is as old as political science itself. It may be found in Aristotle, Lord Bacon, Sir Walter Raleigh, and other writers. Harrington seems, however, to be the first writer who has illustrated and expanded the principle, and given to it the effect and prominence which justly belong to it. To this sentiment, Sir, I entirely agree. It seems to me to be plain, that, in the absence of military force, political power naturally and necessarily goes into the hands which hold the property. In my judgment, therefore, a republican form of government rests, not more on political constitutions, than on those laws which regulate the descent and transmission of property. . . .

"If the nature of our institutions be to found government on property, and that it should look to those who hold property for its protection, it is entirely just that property should have its due weight and consideration in political arrangements. Life and personal liberty are no doubt to be protected by law; but property is also to be protected by law, and is the fund out of which the means for protecting life and liberty are usually furnished. We have no experience that teaches us that any other rights are safe where property is not safe. Confiscation and plunder are generally, in revolutionary commotions, not far before banishment, imprisonment, and death. It would be monstrous to give even the name of government to any association in which the rights of property should not be completely secured. The disastrous revolutions which the world has witnessed, those political thunderstorms and earthquakes which have shaken the pillars of society to their very deepest foundations, have been revolutions against property.

"The English Revolution of 1688 was a revolution in favor of property, as well as of other rights. It was brought about by men of property for their security; and our own immortal Revolution was undertaken, not to shake or plunder property, but to protect it. The acts which the country complained of were such as violated the rights of property. An immense majority of all those who had an interest in the soil were in favor of the Revolution; and they carried it through, looking to its results for the security of their possessions."

In another address, equally cogent, delivered on the anniversary of the landing of the Pilgrims, Webster applied the economic interpretation of politics directly to American institutions. "Our New England ancestors," he said, "brought thither no great capitals from Europe; and if they had, there was nothing productive in which they could have been invested. They left behind them the whole feudal policy of the other continent. . . . They came to a new country. There were as yet no lands yielding rent, and no tenants rendering service. The whole soil was unreclaimed from barbarism. They were themselves either from their original condition, or from the necessity of their common interest, nearly on a general level in respect to property. Their situation demanded a parcelling out and division of the lands, and it may be fairly said that this necessary act *fixed the future frame and form of their government*.[4] The character of their political institutions was determined by the fundamental laws respecting property. . . . The consequence of all these causes has been a great subdivision of the soil and a great equality of condition; the true basis, most certainly, of popular government."

Having thus laid the foundations of politics in economics, Webster went on to give a warn-

[4] Italics are Webster's own.

Doctrines of the Philosophers

ing and a prophecy. "The freest government," he said, "if it could exist, would not be long acceptable, if the tendency of the laws were to create a rapid accumulation of property in few hands and to render the great mass of the population dependent and penniless. In such a case, the popular power must break in upon the rights of property, or else the influence of property must limit and control the exercise of popular power. Universal suffrage, for example, could not long exist in a community where there was great inequality of property. The holders of estates would be obliged in such case either in some way to restrain the right of suffrage, or else such right of suffrage would ere long divide the property."

It is to be regretted that time does not permit the reading of these remarkable speeches in full, but we may summarize all of Webster's conclusions in the following manner:

1. The form of a government is determined (except where the sword rules) by the nature and distribution of property.

2. Republican government rests upon a wide distribution of property, particularly in land.

3. Government to be stable must be founded on men's interest.

4. Property to be secure must have a direct

interest, representation, and check in the government.

5. Disturbances in countries arise principally from the conflict of groups resulting from variations in the form and distribution of property.

6. Universal suffrage is incompatible with great inequality of wealth.

7. Political wisdom requires the establishment of government on property and the control of its distribution through the regulation of alienage and transmission.

Far away in South Carolina, one of Webster's distinguished contemporaries, John C. Calhoun, reached substantially the same conclusions as he pondered upon the rise and fall of states and the problems of statecraft. Like his antagonist in the forum, he had his mind fixed upon the instant need of things—the defence of the special interest of which he was the leading spokesman; but in his quest for power he also sought for the inherent nature of things. Quickly his penetrating glance shot through the texture of political rhetoric to the underlying economic facts.

"If the whole community had the same interests," he declared, "so that the interests of

Doctrines of the Philosophers

each and every portion would be so affected by the action of the government, that the laws which oppressed or impoverished one portion, would necessarily oppress and impoverish all others,—or the reverse,—then the right of suffrage, of itself, would be all-sufficient to counteract the tendency of the government to oppression and abuse of its powers; and, of course, would form, of itself, a perfect constitutional government. The interest of all being the same, by supposition, as far as the action of the government was concerned, all would have like interests as to what laws should be made, and how they should be executed. All strife and struggle would cease as to who should be elected to make and execute them. The only question would be, who was most fit; who the wisest and most capable of understanding the common interest of the whole. This decided, the election would pass off quietly, and without party discord; as no one portion could advance its own peculiar interest without regard to the rest, by electing a favourite candidate.

"But such is not the case. On the contrary, nothing is more difficult than to equalize the action of the government, in reference to the various and diversified interests of the community; and nothing more easy than to pervert its powers into instruments to aggrandize and enrich one or more interests by oppressing and impoverishing the others; and this too, under the operation of laws, couched in general terms;—and which, on their face, appear fair and equal. Nor is this the case in some particular communities only. It is so in all; the small and the great,—the poor and the rich,—irrespective of pursuits, productions, or degrees of civilization;—with, however, this difference, that the more extensive and populous the country, the more diversified the condition and pursuits of its population, and the richer, more luxurious, and dissimilar the people, the more difficult is it to equalize the actions of the government,—and the more easy for one portion of the community to pervert its powers to oppress, and plunder the other.

"Such being the case, it necessarily results, that the right of suffrage, by placing the control of the government in the community must, from the same constitution of our nature which makes government necessary to preserve society, lead to conflict among its different interests,—each striving to obtain possession of its powers, as the means of protecting itself against the others;—or of advancing its respective interests, regardless of the interests of others. For this purpose, a struggle will take place between the various interests to obtain a majority, in order to control the government. If no one interest be strong enough, of itself, to obtain it, a combination will be formed between those whose interests are most alike;—each conceding something to the others, until a sufficient number is obtained to make a majority. The process may be slow, and much time may be required before a compact, organized majority can be thus formed; but formed it will be in time, even without preconcert or design, by the sure workings of that principle or constitution of our nature in which government itself originates. When once formed, the community will be divided into great parties, —a major and a minor,—between which there will be incessant struggles on the one side to retain, and on the other to obtain the majority, —and, thereby, the control of the government and the advantages it confers.

"So deeply seated, indeed, is this tendency to conflict between the different interests or portions of the community, that it would result from the action of the government itself, even though it were possible to find a community, where the people were all of the same pur-

The Economic Basis of Politics

suits, placed in the same condition of life, and in every respect, so situated, as to be without inequality of condition or diversity of interests. The advantages of possessing the control of the powers of the government, and, thereby, of its honours and emoluments, are, of themselves, exclusive of all other consideration, ample to divide even such a community into two great hostile parties."

It is evident from this review that the six great thinkers we have brought under consideration were in substantial agreement on the subject in hand. They believed that the fundamental factors with which the statesman has to deal are the forms and distribution of property and the sentiments and views arising from the possession of different degrees and kinds of property. Upon this generalization, we rest one of two conclusions. We may, upon reflection, decide that the distribution of property is the result of changeless forces inherent in the nature of man, and that the statesman is not a maker but an observer of destiny. Or we may hold that once the forces of social evolution are widely understood man may subdue them to his purposes. He may so control the distribution of wealth as to establish

Doctrines of the Philosophers

an ideal form of society and prevent the
eternal struggle of classes that has shaken so
many nations to their foundations. Man, the
servant of fate, may become the master. But
here we pause. Can the spirit of man be per-
manently enclosed in any system?

II

Economic Groups and the Structure of the State

HAVING surveyed the theories of our six political philosophers, it is fitting and proper that we should inquire whether there has been in fact a close relation between the structure of the state and the economic composition of society. It would be interesting, if time permitted, to examine the constitution of Athens and to consider such matters as Draco's legislation and Solon's reforms or to analyse the illuminating pages in which Polybius describes the balance of powers in Rome. The results of such a study, pondered in connection with the theories we have just reviewed, could not fail to set in train a fascinating line of speculation. There are, however, limits to this undertaking, and we must confine our scrutiny to the modern state in its historical growth.

In reviewing the history of government in

Economic Groups

Western Europe, from the disintegration of the Roman Empire to the opening years of the nineteenth century, we discover that wherever the simple sword-won despotism of the war leader, prince or king, is supplemented or superseded by some form of representation, it is not the people, considered as abstract equal personalities, who are represented, but it is propertied groups, estates. We are told by that profound student of mediaeval law, Dr. Stubbs, that the ideal toward which Europe was slowly working in the middle ages, was a constitution under which each class was admitted to a share of power and control, and national action determined by the balance of forces thus combined.

This was not, as he admits, a conscious design by which statesmen shaped their policies. Many forces and circumstances contributed to the making of the representative system of estates. Sometimes it was the resistance of a particular economic group to royal despotism that won for it a recognized share in the government. An example of this is afforded by the contest which ended in the grant of *Magna Carta*. The barons wrote their interest into the public law of England, and secured it by obtaining the right of actual par-

The Economic Basis of Politics

ticipation as a class in the control of government. At other times kings, especially during wars of conquest or defence, found themselves straitened for funds, and they called upon certain classes or groups of men to fill their treasury. Such, for instance, was the origin of the English House of Commons. To the continued financial necessity of English kings, particularly during the long war with France, was due the extraordinary development in the power of the English Parliament. Whatever the circumstances in each particular case, the striking fact is that we find all over mediaeval Europe what Dr. Stubbs calls, "National assemblies composed of properly arranged and organized classes."

If we examine the constitution of England in the middle ages we find, in fact whatever the theory, four estates: the clergy, the baronage, the landed gentry, and the burgesses. Of these, the first three were founded, in the main, upon landed property. The first or spiritual estate in the English constitution comprised the whole body of the clergy. The clergy were invited to form a part of Parliament for two reasons. Their spiritual power was great, and even the boldest kings did not dare to defy them until the days of the mighty Henry VIII. But it is hardly to be doubted that it was as holders of property of immense value that the clergy came to a large share of the sovereign power. The bishops and the abbots, who were summoned to Parliament by name, were tenants-in-chief of the crown; in other words, they were great landed barons. As such they sat in the House of Lords. The inferior clergy in England, unlike their French brethren, though duly summoned to take their place in the great council of the realm, refused to obey the summons and remained for centuries in a convocation of their own, voting taxes on their property independent of the Parliaments of the realm. Though the clerical order was thus divided, the high authorities of the church sitting in the House of Lords and the inferior clergy dealing with the crown directly, it was mainly as a body of landed proprietors that the spiritual estate shared in the government.

The second English estate was the lay baronage, the members of which sat by their own right in the House of Lords along with the spiritual peers from the clerical estate. It is not necessary to inquire here into the historical circumstances which resulted in drawing a line between the richer barons and the untitled landed gentry, nor into those vainly disputed points of law which have been raised in the search for the origin and exact nature of the property rights which entitled a peer to a seat in the upper House. Whatever the cause may have been, the fact clearly stands forth, as Dr. Stubbs says, that in the middle ages the great land owners, tenants-in-chief, or titled lords, who appeared in person at the Parliament, were separated by a broad line from the freeholders who were represented by the knights of the shire.

According to a custom consecrated by time, it is the fashion to speak of the House of Commons as representing a sort of third estate, the commonalty of the realm. A little antiquarian inquiry, however, shows that the term "commons" does not derive its meaning, as is often erroneously supposed, from any connection with "the common people." On the contrary it comes from the vague word *communitas* which was used in the middle ages to describe a political organism such as a county or chartered town. The House of Commons, therefore, was in reality the house of the *communitates*, composed of representatives of the gentry of the counties and the burgesses of the towns considered as collective bodies within their respective geographical areas. Strictly

[50]

Economic Groups

speaking, we find in the lower house of Parliament the spokesmen of two estates: the smaller landowners and the burgesses. In the early stages of parliamentary evolution, the agents sent by the burgesses were even treated as a separate house or estate, although the way in which they voted on measures is obscure. Later they were combined with the gentry.

It was one of the peculiarities of the English system that the Parliament was not constituted of three or four distinct orders. In France, as we shall see, there were three separate estates —clergy, nobility, and third estate. In Sweden there were four orders—clergy, nobility, burghers, and peasants. In both of these countries each order formed a separate chamber and acted as a collective body. In England, on the other hand, there were only two chambers in the political system, unless we treat the separate convocation of the clergy as a part of the political organism. The House of Lords combined the great landed lay barons with the great landed clerical barons. The House of Commons included burgesses from the towns and representatives of the landed gentry below the baronial line. Still, it is quite apparent, in spite of these combinations that the English constitution of the middle

The Economic Basis of Politics

ages was a group system, resting upon a foundation of economic classes.[1]

The principles underlying this mediaeval system of class representation have never been entirely abandoned in England in favour of the theory of abstract individual equality. They were well understood by Harrington, Locke, and Burke. ✕ Indeed the British constitution of mediaeval origin remained substantially unchanged until 1832, when the first of the great series of parliamentary Reform Bills was enacted. ✕ Although nearly half a century had elapsed since the French Revolution let loose its flood of liberty and equality doctrines, English reformers, even in 1832, remained unmoved. They widened the suffrage, it is true, but what they did in effect was to enfranchise, by a set of ingenious qualifications, another "estate" which had grown up with the advance of industry and commerce, namely, a body of middle class manufacturers and shop keepers. In vain did the English Chartists

*a very sig-
nificant
statement.*

---

[1] It must not be forgotten that the mediæval clergy had a large vested interest in the profession. In addition to the huge landed estates given by pious benefactors for religious purposes, the clergy as a class had a large revenue from fees of various kinds. Much of the opposition of the middle classes to the Catholic Church was economic in origin.

talk of "one man one vote," and universal manhood suffrage.

When the next generation of English reformers "shot Niagara," in 1867, they merely enfranchised another "estate"—the working classes of the great industrial centres. And when again in 1884 a new addition was made to the British constitution, another "estate" was enfranchised, the agricultural labourers. At no point was the tax paying or property notion abandoned by the English in favour of the rule that a man should be allowed to vote simply because he is what Carlyle called "an unfeathered biped."

After the era of individualism set in it was more difficult to trace the line between economic groups than it had been in the middle ages, but whoever reads the debates over the great reform bills in England can see that statesmen, at each period, had in mind not abstract human equality, but what Dr. Stubbs characterized as a constitution in which each class of society should be admitted to a share of power and control. The significance of this story for the political future of England, in view of the changed position of women in industry, particularly since the outbreak of the

[53]

The Thought derived is then that the extention of suffrage has been only on the basis of the extension of property.

Great War, can readily be seen by one who has eyes to see.[2]

Everywhere in mediaeval Europe, as in England, we find constitutions resting upon estates, assemblies representing various orders, classes, and conditions of men, except the rightless serf at the bottom of society. In the Cortes of Aragon sat the clergy, the great barons *(ricos hombres)*, the minor barons or knights, and the burgesses of the towns. The old parliament of Scotland was composed of prelates, barons and the smaller townsmen. In the representative assemblies which sprang up in some German principalities and in Russia, the same idea of class representation prevailed.

In the economic foundations of her Constitution, mediaeval France differed in no fundamental way from the neighboring countries. The history of the French estates, local and general, offers to the student of political science an abundance of group phenomena for analysis and interpretation. The records of more than three hundred years copiously illustrate the

[2] This sentence may stand as written in 1916. Not until 1917, during the great "War for Democracy," did England establish a practically universal suffrage.

Economic Groups

operation of the group process; an added and very significant interest is given to the study by the rôle of the Estates General on the eve of the great Revolution.

As early as 1212, Simon de Montfort called a parliament to which he summoned bishops, nobles, and distinguished bourgeois. A few years later, there was held at Beziers an assembly of the three orders *(des trois ordres)* to give advice relative to provincial administrative organization. In 1254, by royal ordinance, the Seneschal Beaucaire was instructed to take council with the prelates, the barons, the knights, and the representatives of the towns *(hominibus bonarum villarum)*.

The first Estates General, or National Parliament, was held in France in 1303. This was speedily followed by other parliaments. Speaking of the session of 1308, a chronicler said that the king wished to have the advice and consent of men "of every condition in the realm."

Like all early national assemblies, the French Estates General met only on the call of the king, and the methods of election depended naturally upon the terms of the royal orders. Complicated and varying practices were adopted at different times and places, but the

The Economic Basis of Politics

following general principles were commonly observed. The members of the two privileged classes, the high clergy and the nobility, were summoned in person. The important convents and chapters were invited to send delegates. Occasionally the regular and secular clergy of a diocese united to elect their deputies. The nobility of the lower order usually chose their representatives, but sometimes members of this group appeared in person. In the towns the delegates were elected —often under a widely extended suffrage, including, on some occasions, women voters. These orders of society were known collectively as the clergy, the nobility, and the third estate.

It was not thought necessary, however, that each order should be represented only by members of the group. In mediaeval practice, on the contrary, clerks, nobles, curates and canons were sometimes chosen to represent townsmen. Often laymen were selected to speak for the clergy. Again, we see farmers (*roturiers*) and clergy standing as the spokesmen for men of noble order. Again it happened, perhaps to save expense, that the same deputies represented clergy, nobility, and third estate. Whatever the process of selection, however, each class acted separately and developed a certain consciousness of identical interest. When, in 1543, the king sought to unite the three groups in a common election, he found that instead of mitigating the group conflicts he only sharpened them. In a little while he restored the old practice of separate elections.

The French Estates General continued to meet from time to time until 1614, when the last grand session previous to the eve of the Revolution was held. At this memorable meeting there broke out a conflict between the nobility and the third estate which foreshadowed the struggle that was destined, more than one hundred and fifty years later, to destroy the whole system. The violence of this session and perhaps the conflict then raging in England between the Parliament and James I, served as a warning that the monarch should beware of nourishing a dangerous hostility among the national estates.

Whatever may have been the cause—with that we are not now concerned—no session of the Estates General was again called until 1788. In that year the king, being in desperate financial straits, once more summoned the representatives of the different economic groups that could give him relief, to consider the state of the realm. Immediately the antiquarians busied themselves with historical researches in order to restore the ancient and honorable institution in its old form.

To the Estates General of 1789, each estate —clergy, nobility, and third estate—sent its members and representatives. Then arose, as every one knows, a fateful struggle for power. The clergy and nobility, bent on preserving their dominion, insisted that the vote on measures should be taken by the houses, as three distinct orders. Thus they hoped to prevent the upper classes from being overwhelmed by the numerical majority of the third estate, which had twice as many representatives in the assembly as the other two estates combined. Every school history tells us of the deadlock which ensued, of Mirabeau's eloquence, of the Tennis Court Oath, and of the National Assembly which, by firm action, was substituted for the old three-class system. Had the clergy and the nobility been willing earlier to surrender some of their privileges, and concede to the third estate a fair portion of political power, the history of the desperate years that followed the peaceful revolution of 1789 might have been far different. By resisting to the

Economic Groups

breaking point, the clergy and the nobility were conquered and almost destroyed by the third estate.

Less significant for the history of the world, but by no means less interesting in itself, is the parliamentary development of Sweden. From very early times the constitution of that kingdom recognized and provided for the representation of four distinct classes, clergy, nobility, burghers and peasants. In the constitutional reorganization which followed the disturbances of the French Revolution and the Revolutionary Wars, this system was kept intact. Each class was not only distinctly represented, but each class had a house of its own through which the interests of the group were expressed in the government. The great landlords appeared in person. The spiritual house included the bishops and a number of other persons chosen by the clergy, the universities, and the academy of sciences, respectively. The representatives of the middle class were elected by the properly qualified burghers of the towns and the mine owners. The representatives of the peasants were chosen by the landowning farmers and certain other members of the soil-tilling population. Each of the four houses of parliament deliberated alone and acted in the name of and for the class which it represented. Ingenious provisions were devised for obviating deadlocks. This four-class parliament was retained until 1866 when two houses took its place.

The principle of class representation, which had been adopted in the development of mediaeval governments, was taken over entirely by Austria in her constitutional reconstruction shortly after the middle of the nineteenth century. The Austrian upper house consisted, of course, of the nobility, whose economic foundation was the land. In the formation of the lower house, in 1860-1, representation was distributed among the several provinces of the realm and it was provided that the quota to which each province was entitled should be selected by the local legislatures from definite economic groups.

It was stipulated that the total number of deputies to be chosen should be distributed among four distinct "estates," namely, (1) the great landlords (except in Trieste and Vorarlberg where no such class existed, and in Dalmatia where the highest taxpayers were put into this group), (2) the burghers of the cities, markets and industrial places, (3) the

[60]

Economic Groups

peasants of the rural communes, and (4) the chambers of commerce. In 1873 indirect election was abandoned for direct election by popular vote, but the system of class representation remained intact. Twenty-three years later, that is, in 1896, the non-taxpayers and industrial proletariat were admitted to a share in the government. It was provided that seventy-two deputies, now added to the parliament, should be chosen by the voters in general, including those already members of other classes. This system of group representation remained in force until 1907 when manhood suffrage was adopted.

In formulating a constitution after the Revolution of 1848, the King of Prussia deliberately founded his government upon a class system, as you all know from your study of comparative politics. The voters of Prussia are divided into three classes: those who pay one-third of the income taxes elect indirectly one-third of the delegates to the Prussian Diet; those who pay a second third of the income taxes likewise elect a third of the delegates; and finally, all the rest of the voters, who constitute almost the entire electorate, choose the remaining third of the deputies. Thus the Prussian Parliament is made up of

a House of Lords, representing the landed
interests, and a House of Commons or Diet,
representing in two-thirds of its membership
the wealth of the kingdom, and in one-third
the propertyless. Years of agitation and a
threatened revolt on the part of the masses
have failed to shake the foundations of this
strongly knit system of class government.[3]

All this, you may think, is interesting enough,
but without bearing upon American conditions.
It may be said that whatever were the practices of mediaeval France, England, Sweden,
and Aragon, they have no meaning for the
United States founded under another dispensation. There stands the Declaration of Independence with its immortal statement that all
men are born free and equal and that governments derive their just powers from the consent of the governed. Here is what seems to
be a repudiation of the whole notion of class
or group interest in the process of government;
but when we turn from theory to fact we find
ourselves in the midst of mediaeval forms and
institutions.

An examination of the first American state

[3] So things stood in 1916 when these lectures were
given. This system was overthrown in the German Revolution of 1918.

Economic Groups

constitutions reveals no abandonment of the Old-World notion that government rests upon property. Take, for instance, the Massachusetts Constitution of 1780 drawn by John Adams and adopted after long and serious deliberation. In this document we discover that no man could vote for members of the legislature or for governor, unless he had a freehold estate of the annual value of three pounds, or some estate of the value of sixty pounds. Here is a distinct recognition of two classes of property interests in the government, —real property and personalty. To add further security to the two orders or "estates" the constitution provided that no one could be elected governor who did not possess a freehold of the value of one thousand pounds, and furthermore, that the senators should be distributed among the respective districts of the state on the score of the amount of taxes paid in each of them. It was in defence of this last provision that Daniel Webster made his famous speech in the Massachusetts convention of 1820, defending the economic basis of government. If the Massachusetts constitution proved to be rather democratic in its operations, that was, as Webster pointed out, due to the wide distribution of property, not to any desire of the Massachusetts Fathers to sacrifice the security of property to a political shibboleth.

If we take a great middle state like New York, we find that the constitution drafted in 1777 distinctly recognized the existence of classes by establishing the predominance of the farmers. It provided that the senate should be composed of freeholders, and that none but freeholders possessing one hundred pounds worth of land could vote for the senators or for governor. A slighter property qualification was placed upon voters for the lower house—a qualification which admitted freemen of the incorporated towns, renters, and a few others, but kept out the lower levels of the proletariat. This class system remained in vogue until 1821. It was abolished then only against the violent protests of many intellectual leaders of the time, such as Chancellor Kent, who maintained that the rights of property could be protected only when property was frankly represented in the government, and that those "without a stake in the country" should have no voice in its politics.

The Fathers of the South did not differ from those of the North. In the agricultural state of Virginia, where there were few mer-

chants and capitalists, the predominance
which the landed classes possessed in fact was
also established in right. Only freeholders
could vote in that state under the constitution
of 1776, and this restriction was kept in force
for more than half a century. When a vigor-
ous but vain attempt was made, in the constitutional convention of 1829, to abolish it,
the freehold suffrage was defended on the
ground that the landed group was the only
secure foundation for government because all
other classes were variable and transitory in
character, while the possession of land furnished the strongest evidence of permanent,
common interest with, and attachment to, the
community.

Admitting the plain evidence of the first
state constitutions, that the wise founders of
this Republic recognized the place of property
interests in political processes, it may be said
that the Constitution of the United States,
drawn in that period, nowhere takes into account the existence of economic divisions.
This is true, if we read merely the language of
the instrument and not the records of the convention which drafted it. In the document itself there are no provisions similar to those
which appear in the first state constitutions,

placing landed- and personal-property qualifications on the suffrage and office holding; but the omission was not made because the framers of that immortal instrument were indifferent to the rights of property or unaware of the influence wielded by economic groups upon the course of government. Neither was it because they disapproved of property qualifications, for such existed in nearly every state in the Union. In fact property qualifications for officers and for voters were proposed in the convention, but it was impossible to agree on their precise form. Inasmuch as many of the troubles under the Articles of the Confederation had arisen from attacks on capital by state legislatures elected by freeholders, and inasmuch as the convention was especially eager to safeguard the rights of personal property, a freehold qualification did not seem to offer an adequate remedy. On the other hand, to impose a large personal-property qualification on voters would have meant the defeat of the Constitution by the farmers who were, of necessity, called upon to ratify it. Under the circumstances the framers of the Constitution relied, not upon direct economic qualifications, but upon checks and balances to secure the rights of property—particularly personal

[66]

Economic Groups

property—against the assaults of the farmers and the proletariat.[4]

At this point we may summarize. Our six political philosophers regarded property, in its various forms and distribution, and the social groups which arise out of economic processes, as the fundamental materials for the science of government. We have seen also that the constitutions of government of great nations were, for centuries, deliberately fitted to the division of society into separate orders, groups, and estates, each of which pursued a separate calling and cherished its own sentiments about economic interests.

This great fact stands out clearly, that through the centuries—down until our own day—group interests were recognized as forming the very essence of politics both in theory and practice. Statesmen spoke of them, negotiated with them, placated them, legislated for them, and sought sometimes to secure the predominance of one or the other or the balance of several against one or another. At all events, statesmen spoke not of abstract men and abstract rights, but of real men and real rights. What has happened to sweep away the practices

[4] This subject is covered at length in my *Economic Interpretation of the Constitution*, pp. 152-168.

of centuries, to challenge the philosophy of the world's greatest political thinkers, and to introduce the rule of "the people" instead of the rule of estates? Have the economic conditions of the world been revolutionized, the estates and orders abolished?

III

The Doctrine of Political Equality

THE great political philosophers, with few exceptions, have regarded property as the fundamental element in political power, and have looked upon a constitution as a balance of economic groups. The governments founded and developed before the nineteenth century were in fact complexes of group interests. Nowhere was the representative system, in its origin, designed to reflect the opinions of mere numerical aggregations of human beings considered in the abstract apart from property and employment. On the contrary, it reflected the sentiments and views of different sorts and conditions of men, estates or orders: clergy, nobility, burghers, and peasants.

In the United States where there was no clerical estate or established nobility to be represented in the government, the existence of the two fundamental property groups—the owners of realty and the owners of personalty—was

[69]

taken into account either in positive constitutional law or in the check and balance system provided by the separation of powers.[1] If the first American constitutions were more democratic than those of Europe, the fact is not to be attributed to radical changes in human nature, induced by a voyage across the Atlantic, but, as the great Webster pointed out, to a very wide distribution of property, due mainly to cheap land.

So things stood in the closing years of the old régime. Then suddenly came two great revolutions, one in economic fact, and the other in political theory. The first was brought about by the invention of the steam engine and machinery, creating an immense amount of property which had hitherto existed only as a minor element in economic life, namely, industrial and mercantile capital. So rapidly did this new form of property accumulate that even in the United States, by the middle of the nineteenth century, it exceeded in value the agricultural land of the country.

[1] Much ingenuity has been spent by American lawyers in elaborating the theoretical fictions of Montesquieu. The real significance of the separation of powers and its relation to the balance of class interests in society was appreciated by eighteenth century writers, but if more modern statesmen have understood them they have never been frank in setting forth their views.

Doctrine of Political Equality

Being more mobile and more easily concentrated than land, a vast portion of it quickly fell into the hands of, relatively speaking, a small portion of society. As land was the great stabilizer of the old order, so capital became the great disturber in the new order. Like a mighty giant tossing to and fro in a fever, in its quest for profits, it tore masses of men from the land, from their sleepy villages and hamlets, and hurled them here and there all over the globe. Under its influence the old sharp class differences were disarranged. The peasant might become a successful cotton spinner, a financial magnate, a contributor to party war-chests, a peer of the realm. The Manchester individualists, Cobden and Bright, looking upon the new order which they had helped to create, pronounced it good and declared that because any hustling individual might rise from poverty to wealth, the era of *individual* equality had arrived. Instead of studying the new groups, the new class divisions, more subtle and complex than ever before, they proclaimed the glad day of equality.

While James Watt was experimenting in Glasgow with the steam engine, and thus preparing to blow up the old economic order in the realm of fact, a French philosopher, Jean

The Economic Basis of Politics

Jacques Rousseau, was experimenting with ideas scarcely less dangerous to the *ancien régime* than the operations of the Scotch mechanic. Unlike his distinguished predecessor in political science, Montesquieu, Rousseau did not search assiduously among the institutions and habits of mankind to find a basis for his political philosophy.[2] Rousseau was not a man of science or a detached scholar. He was a passionate propagandist. He formulated

[2] Montesquieu recognized the place of economic groups in his system of political economy:

"In a popular state the inhabitants are divided into certain classes. It is in the manner of making this division that great legislators have signalized themselves; and it is on this the duration and prosperity of democracy have ever depended. Servius Tullius followed the spirit of aristocracy in the distribution of his classes. We find in Livy and in Dionysius Halicarnassus, in what manner he lodged the right of suffrage in the hands of the principal citizens. He had divided the people of Rome into a hundred and ninety-three centuries, which formed six classes; and ranking the rich, who were in smaller numbers, in the first centuries; and those in middling circumstances, who were more numerous, in the next, he flung the indigent multitude into the last; and as each century had but one vote, it was property rather than numbers that decided the elections. Solon divided the people of Athens into four classes. In this he was directed by the spirit of democracy, his intention not being to fix those who were to choose, but such as were eligible: therefore, leaving to every citizen the right of election, he made the judges eligible from each of those four classes; but the magistrates he ordered to be chosen only out of the first three, consisting of persons of easy fortunes."—Montesquieu, *The Spirit of Laws,* Vol I, p. 10.

the sentiments and views of the third estate in France then beginning to thunder against the monarchy, which was buttressed by the special privileges of the clergy and the nobility. In his *Social Contract* he set forth the moral and philosophic justification for the revolt of the third estate.

In his system of political thought, Rousseau, in effect, advanced several negative propositions. He denied that there was any inherent and essential connection between economics and politics. He repudiated the idea that the nature and amount of men's material possessions and the character of their occupations could have any substantial influence on their political sentiments and their political actions. He rejected the age long view that the transmission, alienation, accumulation, and distribution of wealth bore a fundamental relation to the form and practices of the government. He denied the doctrine that society is a complex of more or less conscious groups and interests. For the group- or class-man he substituted the abstract, the cosmopolitan, the universal man.

In order that we may get the essence of this new political philosophy, let us make a somewhat close examination of the doctrines laid

The Economic Basis of Politics

down by Rousseau. He simply cannot be ignored, for his *Social Contract* became the text book of the French Revolution and of that world wide equalizing movement which has in our day penetrated even the heart of China, preparing the way for the overthrow of absolutism and the triumph of the third estate.

The origin of the state Rousseau finds not in a divine command that one should rule over others, or in the fusion of estates, but in a voluntary union of free men. Of course Rousseau knows that this was not true, in point of fact, and respect for the truth compels him to admit it. But he cannot allow the matter of historicity to interfere with the foundations of his system of political ethics.

In Book I of his *Social Contract,* he says: "If, then, we remove from the social contract all that is not of its essence, it will be reduced to the following terms: Each of us gives in common his person and all his force under the supreme direction of the general will; and we receive each member as an indivisible part of the whole.

"Immediately, this act of association produces, instead of the individual person of each contracting party, a moral and collective body, composed of as many members as the assembly

[74]

Doctrine of Political Equality

has votes, which receives from the same act its utility,—its common being, its life and its will. This public personage, thus formed by the union of all the others, formerly took the name of city, and now takes that of republic or body politic. This is called the *state* by its members when it is passive; the *sovereign* when it is active; and a *power* when comparing it to its equals. With regard to the associates, they take collectively the name *people,* and call themselves individually *citizens,* as participating in the sovereign authority, and *subjects,* as submitted to the laws of the state. But these terms are often confounded and are taken one for the other. It is enough to know how to distinguish them when they are employed with all precision."

Having found the origin of society in a general agreement of free and equal men, Rousseau naturally places sovereign power by moral right in "the people"—a collectivity of all the individual members of the state. The law of the state is therefore not the will of some class (like the landed gentry) imposed upon all others, or a compromise rule produced by a balance of conflicting group interests, but is, according to Rousseau, an expression of "the general will." This alone is its justification.

The Economic Basis of Politics

If it destroys the rights and property of the individual still he must abide by it. "In order then that the social contract may not be an idle formula, it includes tacitly this engagement, which alone can give force to the others, that whoever shall refuse to obey the general will, shall be compelled to it by the whole body. This signifies nothing if not that he will be forced to be free; for it is this condition which, giving each citizen to the country, guarantees him from all personal dependence—a condition which forms the device and working of the political machine, and alone renders legitimate civil engagements which without that would be absurd, tyrannical, and subject to great abuse."

In the formulation of this general will, all individuals share alike. Here Rousseau proclaims the doctrine of absolute political equality with a vengeance. If the state, he says, is composed of ten thousand citizens, then each member of the state has one ten-thousandth part of the sovereign authority. If the people is composed of one hundred thousand men, then the citizen's suffrage is reduced to a hundred-thousandth part, and he has obviously ten times less influence in the formation of the laws. Hence it follows, declares the philoso-

Doctrine of Political Equality

pher, "that the larger the state becomes, the less liberty there is."

But Rousseau is face to face with the fact that unanimity among citizens is impossible and that the general will cannot be the will of the whole ten thousand or the whole hundred thousand, as the case may be, but must, perforce, be the will of a certain fraction of the citizens. He boldly meets the problem, and following the old philosophers he holds that the exercise of sovereignty is by the majority. The *general will* of which he makes so much, is in practice, the will of a majority. With fine confidence he contends that the will of the majority is right and works for the good of the state. The minority is wrong; it is nothing, because it follows from the nature of the social contract that the minority must accept the decrees of the majority. With the courage of his convictions, he says: "When, however, the opinion contrary to mine prevails, it only shows that I was mistaken, and that what I had supposed to be the general will was not general. If my individual opinion had prevailed, I should have done something other than I had intended, and then I should not have been free."

As he contemplates the consequences of this bold doctrine Rousseau shrinks a bit. There

is a limit even to the self-abnegation of the re-
former. In Chapter VI of the Fourth Book
Rousseau safeguards the oppressed minority
in certain fundamental matters by requiring an
extraordinary majority of two-thirds—even
three-fourths in some cases. But this is rather
an afterthought, though a very serious one.
It does not vitally affect his extreme doctrines
of individualization. Neither did it check
materially the fateful consequences of his general doctrine of universal male equality.
Rousseau is aware of the dangers of mere numerical majorities, but he cannot escape al-
together the results of his general levelling
down. There is simply a limit to which he can
allow the logic of his argument to carry him.
Just as he excludes women from his "people"
so he sets some metes and bounds to the doings
of the mere majority.[3]

Nothing further need be said to show how
revolutionary was Rousseau's doctrine for the
old order, or for any order. Under it the
rights and property of all groups and all classes

[3] Aulard contends that Rousseau was a *bourgeois* and in
reality wished to exclude the propertyless as well as the
women from his "people." Whether this is true or not,
Rousseau's disciples, in the earlier stages of the Revolution,
were not ready to throw away all property qualifications
on the suffrage.

become subject to the will of the numerical majority. Any system of government founded on a compromise, or a balance of interest, in defiance of mere numbers on the one side or the other, thus becomes not only indefensible, but immoral and undemocratic. Written to exalt the individual, it subjects him to a new tyranny —the will of a temporary majority. For his sufferings in conscience or in property, it offers him the consoling information that his individual will, being contrary to the general will, is wrong, and, in fact, not his intention at all!

Indeed, as we look at this system, it seems so unreal, so ill-adapted to the world of industry and trade, commerce and agriculture, that its implications are astounding. We can hardly imagine how it could become the philosophy of any people. An examination into the course of events, however, makes the explanation clear.

Naturally enough Rousseau's philosophy did not appeal to the French clergy and nobility, who were aware of their class interests and of their numerical inferiority. To them the social contract was poisonous and impious anarchy.

To the bourgeois, on the other hand, it pre-

sented a different aspect. They had grown
powerful in numbers and wealth, and they
felt keenly the oppressive privileges enjoyed by
the clergy and nobility. They were determined
to sweep away the discriminations against
them, and to control the government in their
own interests. If they did not contemplate the
destruction of the clergy and the nobility as
classes, they did contemplate levelling them
down in their political and economic privileges.
The clergy and the nobility had a monopoly of
the philosophy of divine right—the moral support of their power. The bourgeois had to
look elsewhere for a philosophy to justify such
levelling as they contemplated. They found it
in Rousseau's *Social Contract*. Searching for
an ethical support for their attack upon two
powerful groups, they exalted "the people" as
against all special privileges. They were play-
ing with fire and they knew it, but there seemed
no other philosophy at hand to serve as a foil
for their enterprise. Unwittingly they started
a conflict, the consequences of which will last
until the end of time.

In the shock of the French Revolution the
bourgeois overthrew the nobility and the
clergy. They abolished the feudal rights of
the former and seized the property of the

Doctrine of Political Equality

latter. In their fear of the privileged orders they established a legislature of one chamber and sought to safeguard their property by a tax-paying qualification on the right to vote; but the logic of their position was fatal. They had proclaimed the rights of man as the moral justification for the destruction of the rights of two classes, and they had at the same time coolly repudiated the rights of man by limiting the application of the doctrine to their own class.

Then followed the Revolution of violence and terror in which radical leaders inflamed the disfranchised by appeals to the gospel of Rousseau and to the proclamations of the bourgeois. To save themselves the latter had to resort to that other great source of authority, the sword. This instrument was wielded by Napoleon Bonaparte, a man who understood the relation of property to political power, and who, through his constitutions based on checks and balances, gave stability to bourgeois institutions. Even Napoleon, the Bourbons, and the Orleanists, however, could not stay the onward march of Rousseau and his legions.[4]

[4] In the Declaration of the Rights of Man—August 1789—the French National Assembly proclaimed in theory the political philosophy of Rousseau: "men are born and remain equal in rights," and "law is the expression of

The Economic Basis of Politics

But it may be asked, how did this levelling doctrine of universal political equality find a foothold in the United States where there were no official clergy and nobility to be overthrown by the third estate? Well, some writers have laboured hard to show that it is a French creation utterly at variance with Anglo-Saxon tradition—whatever that may mean. In the interest of truth, however, it should be said that the free-and-equal doctrine is not French, but English in origin. Its beginnings among English-speaking peoples may be traced to the flood of speculation that broke loose in England during the seventeenth century when the merchants and gentry were engaged in a revolt against the crown and aristocracy—the clergy having been broken a century earlier by the bluff king, Henry VIII, who confiscated much of their property. It was from English defenders of revolution, like John Locke, rather than from French authors, that Jefferson derived the gospel of the Declaration of Inde-

the general will." In the National Assembly it appears that only five deputies, however, asked for universal manhood suffrage—among them Robespierre, who was destined to ride the storm of the proletarian revolution which he fain would have tempered with a pale and sickly piety. It is estimated that under the first French Constitution about three-fifths of the adult males were deprived of the suffrage by the property qualifications established. Thus did the bourgeois mutilate the doctrines of Jean Jacques.

Doctrine of Political Equality

pendence. Moreover the economic circumstances in the United States were on the whole favorable to the propaganda of that word. There was no established clergy here. There was no titled aristocracy. There was no such proletariat as formed the "mob" of Paris. Land was the chief form of property and its wide distribution among the whites (leaving the slaves out of account) brought about in fact a considerable economic equality to correspond to the theory of political equality.

Moreover, at the time that America was committed to the theory of political equality, the people were engaged in a revolt against the government imposed on them under the authority of Great Britain. Like the third estate in France they needed some effective and compelling justification for their extraordinary conduct. Of course the leaders of the American Revolution could have said coldly: "We are fighting for the plantation owners of the South, the merchants and landed gentry of the North, and the free farmers in both sections, in order that they may govern themselves."

Obviously, such a chilly declaration of fact would not have thrilled the masses, especially the mechanics of the towns who enjoyed no political rights under either system, the old or the new. It was necessary to have something that would ring throughout the country. Hence the grand words of the Declaration of Independence: "All men are created equal" and "governments derive their just powers from the consent of the governed." There were critics ready to point out that these high principles did not square with slavery, indentured servitude, and political disfranchisement, but they did not prevail. In the fervour of the moment, Jefferson, while bent on justifying the revolt against George III, in fact challenged the rule of property which was guaranteed by the state constitutions drafted by his fellow revolutionists in that very epoch. Even Jeffersonians, when confronted, like Rousseau's followers, with the logical consequences of their doctrine shrank from applying it. Nevertheless the grand words stood for all time, and advocates of manhood suffrage and woman suffrage afterward appealed to them with great effect in attacking property and sex qualifications on the right to vote.

When once the free-and-equal doctrine had been let loose in the New World and the Old, it was impossible to check its course. Steadily it made headway against governments founded

Doctrine of Political Equality

upon a class basis. Steadily it supplanted the old philosophy of politics which gave to property and to estates a place in the process of government. Within seventy years after the Declaration of Independence the battle for white manhood suffrage was virtually won in the United States. Some remnants of the old system of class privilege in politics remained, but they were regarded as anachronisms. Time was to dispose of them. America was committed to the great doctrine that in politics all heads are equal and all are entitled to the same share of power in the government.

In Europe also political equalitarianism has done deadly work in the old order. In England it has not been carried to the same degree as in the United States, but the Lords' Veto Act, levelling down the power of the ancient and honourable Chamber of Peers, is an echo of it, full of significance for the future.[5] In Sweden, in 1866, the four-class system was swept away in favour of a general suffrage. Austria abandoned group representation in 1907. The

[5] The suffrage act of 1917 passed after this was written carried England into Rousseau's camp. The revolution that followed the German defeat in 1918 swept Germany and the new continental states into the main current. Russia, however, went back to the class system while attempting to abolish the clergy, the nobility, and the bourgeois as classes.

The Economic Basis of Politics

third French Republic abolished the Chamber
of Peers and substituted a Senate, now chosen
by indirect election. At this moment China is
in the throes of a Revolution due to the struggle
between those who would establish a stable
government on the foundations of effective economic and military interests, and those fired
with a passion for "the rights of man."

The logical application of Rousseau's doctrine of complete and abstract human equality
is clear. It means that the number of members
in any legislature shall be apportioned among
geographical districts approximately according
to the number of inhabitants without reference
to their wealth, occupations, or interests. It
means that all high public officers shall be
elected by majorities or pluralities. Man is to
be regarded as a "political" animal. No account is to be taken of those sentiments and
views which, as Madison says, arise from the
possession of different degrees and kinds of
property. All heads are equal and, from the
point of view of politics, alike. The statesman is a mathematician concerned with counting heads. The rule of numbers is enthroned.
The homage once paid to kings is to be paid
to the statistics of election returns. Surely,

in all the history of thought, there is nothing more wonderful than this.

While this political revolution has been going on, have the economic groups once recognized by statesmen and political philosophers disappeared? The answer is emphatic. It is to be found in the census returns, which, as certainly as the doomsday book of William the Conqueror, record the perdurance of group and class interests despite the rhetoric of political equality. It is to be found in practical politics day by day. Does any one think that a thousand farmers or labourers, going on about their tasks, have the same influence in the formation of a protective tariff bill as a thousand manufacturers represented by spokesmen in the lobbies and committee rooms of the Congress of the United States? Does any one suppose that the exemption of trade unions from the provisions of the Sherman Anti-Trust Law was the result of the platonic wishes of "the people," rather than the determined and persistent activity of The American Federation of Labor?

We are therefore confronted by an inherent antagonism between our generally accepted political doctrines, and the actual facts of political life. In the world of natural science men do not tarry long with hypotheses that will not square with observed phenomena. Shall we in the field of political science cling to a delusion that we have to deal only with an abstract man divorced from all economic interests and group sentiments?

IV

The Contradiction and the Outcome

THREE general conclusions were reached in the preceding chapters. A survey of six great systems of political philosophy supports the proposition that there is a vital relation between the forms of state and the distribution of property, revolutions in the state being usually the results of contests over property. A study of the evolution of government in western civilization during many centuries shows the recognition of economic classes in the creation of political organisms. Finally, modern equalitarian democracy, which reckons all heads as equal and alike, cuts sharply athwart the philosophy and practice of the past centuries.

Nevertheless, the democratic device of universal suffrage does not destroy economic classes or economic inequalities. It ignores them. Herein lies the paradox, the most astounding political contradiction that the world

The Economic Basis of Politics

has ever witnessed. Hence the question arises: Has political democracy solved the problem of the ages, wrung the answer from the sphinx? Is it a guarantee against the storms of revolution? Does it make impossible such social conflicts as those which tore ancient societies asunder? Does it afford to mankind a mastery over its social destiny?

To ask these questions is to answer them.[1] Nothing was more obvious in the thinking of western civilization before the outbreak of the World War than dissatisfaction with political democracy. Equally obvious was the discontent with representative government based on the doctrine of abstract numbers and civic equality. Whether one went into the countryside of Oregon or strolled along Quai d'Orsay, one heard lively debates over "the failure of representative government." The initiative and referendum and recall—direct government —more head counting on the theory of numbers and abstract equality, such was the answer of the Far West to the riddle. Europe had another answer, or rather many other answers.

Indeed, John Stuart Mill, in his work on representative government published in 1859, nearly ten years before the radical suffrage

[1] This lecture has been re-written since the close of the World War, but the main conclusions have not been altered.

[90]

Contradiction and the Outcome

measure of 1867, sensed grave dangers ahead.
He utterly rejected the theory that political
democracy would inevitably avoid those acts
of selfishness and arbitrary power that had
characterized monarchies and oligarchies and
aristocracies. "Looking at democracy in the
way in which it is commonly conceived," he
said, "as the rule of the numerical majority,
it is surely possible that the ruling power may
be under the dominion of sectional or class interests pointing to conduct different from that
which would be dictated by impartial regard
for the interest of all. . . . In all countries
there is a majority of poor, a minority who, in
contradistinction, may be called rich. Between
these two classes, on many questions, there is
a complete opposition of interest. We will
suppose the majority sufficiently intelligent to
be aware that it is not to their advantage to
weaken the security of property, and that it
would be weakened by any act of arbitrary
spoliation. But is there not considerable danger lest they should throw upon the possessors
of what is called realizable property and upon
larger incomes, an unfair share, or even the
whole of the burden of taxation; and having
done so, add to the amount without scruple,
expending the proceeds in modes supposed to

conduce to the profit and advantage of the labouring class?" Mill then goes on to cite other examples of the possible abuse of political power in the interests of the economic classes.

His solution of the problem was a balance of classes and the introduction of minority or proportional representation. "If the representative system could be made ideally perfect," he said, "and if it were possible to maintain it in that state, its organization should be such that these two classes, manual labourers and their affinities on one side, employers of labour and their affinities on the other, should be, in the arrangement of the representative system, equally balanced, each influencing about an equal number of votes in Parliament." The more rational minority in each class should then hold the balance. "Assuming that the majority of each class, in any differences between them, would be mainly governed by their class interests, there would be a minority of each in whom that consideration would be subordinate to reason, justice, and the good of the whole; and this minority of either joining with the whole of the other, would turn the scale against any demands of their own majority which were not such as ought to prevail."

Whether this solution is fanciful or sound need not detain us now. The point is that this learned and sincere friend of democracy, writing at the middle of the nineteeth century, believed that the introduction of "numerical democracy" had not solved and could not solve the most fundamental of all contradictions: namely the contests over property and the distribution of wealth that accompany the development of civilization. Indeed Mill's very solution, minority representation, in effect was designed to re-introduce, without rigid legal divisions, the scheme of class representation which had been for centuries the basis of all parliamentary systems. On the significance of this it is not necessary to comment.

Long after Mill's day a group of continental writers, Leon Duguit, Charles Benoist, and Albert Schaeffle, for example, declared the system of artificial territorial divisions and numerical majorities to be a sham and a delusion, and advocated the frank and legal recognition of commerce, industry, property, professions, and crafts in the constitution of the representative system. They held that the

[93]

doctrine of abstract equality was essentially false and in plain contradiction to the facts of modern social life. They declared that it made the politician a sort of broker (hardly an honest one at that) mediating between conflicting groups and slipping into parliament by deluding electors with phrases, promises, and rhetoric. Thus, in their opinion, the state had passed from the hands of practical and informed men of affairs into the control of the "politicians"—men without any business qualifications whose stock in trade was oratory. Thus they could only see disaster ahead, unless the rhetoricians were expelled and representation restored to the basis of economic realities.

Even more savage in their criticism of numerical democracy and abstract political equality were the socialists. They also declared that the idea of political equality and economic inequality contained an inherent contradiction. They offered however, a drastic solution—the ownership of all productive property by society and the consequent destruction of both the capitalist class and the working class. The guild socialists, as another school was called, proposed to substitute for the system of numerical and territorial representation a congress composed of delegates from the various

Contradiction and the Outcome

craft or trade unions. Still other socialists, fearing the disruptive effects of craft jealousies, insisted that at least one branch of the parliament should represent the people considered as a national unity as distinguished from the people divided into crafts and unions. These last reformers argued that man was a civic and patriotic animal and that his whole nature was not expressed or exhausted in his capacity as an engineer, machinist, or farmer.

All these schemes, however, remained devices on paper until the communist upheaval in Russia in November, 1917. Then the world witnessed the attempt to abolish class antagonisms by the nationalization of land and industrial capital. At the same time the idea of political democracy was denounced and cast aside as a mere "bourgeois" device calculated to delude the working class. In the place of a congress of representatives chosen by equal suffrage from territorial districts having substantially the same number of inhabitants, there was established a soviet or council representing economic groups as such. Whatever may be the outcome of this upheaval, we must admit that it was a simple and drastic attempt to dispose of the contradiction between political theory and economic facts.

The Economic Basis of Politics

The experiment has been carried on long enough for us now to observe certain general tendencies. The first is that the nationalization of the land was a mere gesture; the peasants with their feet on the soil remain in possession of it in spite of parchment and seals. The destruction of the soil-tilling, soil-owning peasant by violence was an utter failure. "Nothing could be more stupid," said Lenine in March, 1919, "than the idea even of employing violence against the small owning peasant class engaged in agricultural exploitation." So the Russian Bolshevists fell back upon a plan of converting the peasant to communism by showing that co-operative labour on the land was more productive. At best that was a millennial undertaking. So the communist order had to reckon with one powerful propertied class.

Without now considering the prophecy that the capitalist class will be restored in Russia under some kind of state socialist design, we may take note of certain tendencies in the working class movement itself. In the first place the operation of the communist system called into being an enormous managerial bureaucracy. According to estimates by Mr. Zinoviev published in July, 1920, approximately

[96]

Contradiction and the Outcome

one fourth the adults in Petrograd were government officials and another fourth were sol-
diers. It does not require very much research
to discover many signs of conflict and jealousy
between the industrial workers and the soft-
handed occupants of swivel-chairs.

That is not all. There have been all
along conflicts between the craft unions of
skilled workers and the communists who were
wont to speak of all workers as abstractions,
alike and equal. The contention of the communists was of course as great a fiction as the
theory of political equality.

When the communists ceased to be mere
opponents of capitalists and were charged with
management, they soon discovered the un-
reality of their rhetoric. They likewise discovered the futility of the hope that a system
of equality in pay would draw forth vast productive energies. Therefore, they were compelled to negotiate with craft unions and to
reward skill and talent with extra remuneration.
Of course, they said that this was all temporary
and merely an introduction to the postponed
millennium. That may be, but viewing politics
from the standpoint of an experimental science,
we cannot take into serious account dreams un-
realized.

The Economic Basis of Politics

The upshot of all this seems to be that in a modern industrial society, the problem of property, so vital in politics, is not as simple as it was in old agricultural societies. It was one thing for peasants to destroy their landlords and go on tilling the soil as they had long been wont to do. It is another thing for workingmen to destroy capitalists as a class and assume all the complex and staggering burdens of management and exchange. It is also clear that, as efficient production depends to a great extent upon skill, skill itself is a form of property even if property in capital is abolished.

In short a great society, whether capitalist or communist, must possess different kinds and grades of skill and talent and carry on widely diversified industries. There must be miners, machinists, electricians, engineers, accountants, transport workers, draftsmen, managers, and a hundred other kinds of specialists. They may be temporarily welded together in a conflict with their capitalist employers, but they will be divided over the distribution of wealth among themselves after the capitalists have been disposed of. Conceivably a highly militarist government might destroy their organizations and level them down, but the result would be the ruin of production and of the state itself. Even a communist could hardly defend his system on the theory that all must choose between military despotism and utter ruin.

The grand conclusion, therefore, seems to be exactly that advanced by our own James Madison in the Tenth Number of the Federalist. To express his thought in modern terms: a landed interest, a transport interest, a railway interest, a shipping interest, an engineering interest, a manufacturing interest, a public-official interest, with many lesser interests, grow up of necessity in all great societies and divide them into different classes actuated by different sentiments and views. The regulation of these various and interfering interests, whatever may be the formula for the ownership of property, constitutes the principal task of modern statesmen and involves the spirit of party in the necessary and ordinary operations of government. In other words, there is no rest for mankind, no final solution of eternal contradictions. Such is the design of the universe. The recognition of this fact is the beginning of wisdom—and of statesmanship.

A splendid little book.
Full of material for
Thoughts & meditation

Finished
12-25-'23 - at Norman.